The Language of Spring

To Gisela....
who is Spring to
us in any season.
Merry Christmas
and love,
    Sally, Kerry &
    Wynne

The

Poems for the Season of Renewal

Language

Selected by Robert Atwan

of

Introduction by Maxine Kumin

Spring

Beacon Press · Boston

BEACON PRESS
25 Beacon Street
Boston, Massachusetts 02108–2892
www.beacon.org

Beacon Press books are published under the auspices of
the Unitarian Universalist Association of Congregations.

This book is printed on acid-free paper that meets the uncoated
paper ANSI/ NISO specifications for permanence as revised in 1992.

Text design by Christopher Kuntze
Composed in Sabon and Bickham Script types

LIBRARY OF CONGRESS CATALOGING-IN-PUBLICATION DATA IS AVAILABLE

CONTENTS

Introduction: Easing the Spring

Mary Oliver, in her poem titled "Spring," describes a bear sow newly awake on the mountian "in the brisk and shallow restlessness / of early spring . . . her four black fists / flicking the gravel . . . " Seeing her as an emblem of the natural world we celebrate moves Oliver to raise the issue that the work in this anthology attempts to answer: "There is only one question: / How to love this world." Frost, too, in his almost simplistic lyric, "A Prayer in Spring," after praising all the perquisites of the season, declares, "For this is love and nothing else is love. . . ."

Certainly, of the four seasons, spring is the easiest to love. It opens invitingly, especially here in New England after an often prodigious winter, promising relief from snow and sleet and nightly below-zero readings. Sap runs, streams thaw, dirt roads go glutinous with often impassable mud. Trout season opens. Robins reappear, often on lawns newly dusted with late snow . . . The horses begin to shed their winter coats, wiry threads that turn up later lining the neat nests of chickadees. It's a time of new lambs. Calves and fawns are born.

And as daily temperatures edge upward, the pale greens of grassland and the red tips of skeletal trees before they leaf out promise lushness to come. Although, in Elizabeth Bishop's "A Cold Spring," ". . . the violet was flawed on the lawn," the dogwood is approaching apotheosis. Bishop lifts us out of our chairs with this unexpected description of its blossoms: ". . . each petal burned, apparently, by a cigarette butt."

By contrast, here and there stand Housman's genteel "[L]oveliest of trees, the cherry now ... " and Whitman's "apple orchards, the trees all cover'd with blossoms. . . ." May Sarton delights in the arrival of new leaves: "Small open parasols of Chinese green ... " Even the often acerbic Philip Larkin reports, "The trees are coming into leaf / Like something almost being said ... " and Jane Kenyon notes, in her neighbor's fresh activity, "the soundlessness of winter / give way to hammering."

There is something typically British in Hopkins's boyhood memory, when robbing birds' nests was almost a rite of passage for adolescent boys. He tells us, "Thrush's eggs look little low heavens." But the Jesuit's terse admonition follows, with stresses on all three verbs: "Have, get, before it cloy," and this acknowledgment of spring's brevity overlaying human depravity too is a recurring theme in this collection.

Perhaps its best example is Henry Reed's "Naming of Parts." This World War II poem is frequently overlooked by contemporary anthologists, doubtless on grounds that it is anachronistic in a culture of war conducted by air rather than ground troops. Reed's infantry recruits must learn how to use "the lower sling swivel" and "the bolt" and "the breech," which leads him to this verbal play: "Easing the spring. And rapidly backwards and forward / The early bees are assaulting and fumbling the flowers: / They call it easing the Spring." Is this poem to facile for today's bright readers? Possibly. Nevertheless, I treasure it.

Everywhere I look, spring is being eased. Spring is a story never fully told, a topic to be approached from many vantage points. Sorrow, anger, loss—Louise Bogan proclaims that she is an old hand at grief: "It is not now I learn / To turn the heart away / From the rain of the wet May / Good for the grass and leaves."

We readers expect William Carlos Williams's widow in "The Widow's Lament in Springtime" to grieve her loss in his sparing yet telling details, but nothing prepares us for the stark conclusion in which she contemplates suicide: "I feel that I would like / to go there / and fall into those flowers / and sink into the marsh near them."

Sara Teasdale—hurrah for the inclusion of her seldom-heard voice!—turns the identification of poet or persona with the season upside down. Although it is wartime, she lists the usual touchstones of spring, "... soft rains and the smell of the ground, / And swallows circling with their shimmering sound ..." but concludes that nature is completely indifferent to man's fate. "Not one would mind, neither bird nor tree / If mankind perished utterly. ..."

On the contrary, Lizette Woodworth Reese (another fine poet, rarely heard from, of that period), declares that, far from indifferent, spring insists on her participation: "For certainly it will rush in at last, / And in my own house seize me at its will, / And drag me out to the white fury there." And A. R. Ammons laments that he came too late to see it, but he too hears the season's directive: "don't worry, said the mountain, / try the later nothern slopes / or if / you can climb, climb / into spring. . . ."

Modern poets are not often likely to take such chances with personification. They are for the most part wary of linking spring with passion. Too romantic. Love-dove, fire-desire. Too sentimental. Stale, clichéd, used up, overdone. The reader will have to look back to redoubtable Amy Lowell for this lost art of total immersion. She took the plunge in "Vernal Equinox," moving from "[t]he scent of hyacinths" and "the thrusting of green shoots" to rant in the last line, "Why are you not here to overpower me with your tense and urgent love?"

If spring is a season of hope, of new beginning, if it speaks of resurrection of the spirit and rebirth from the soild, it also projects a tart note that seems particularly congenial to contemporary poets. Jame Tate bids farewell to winter, to seclusion, and wanders "this spring in my disguises." But "[t]he further I delve into these murderous zones / the more crisscrossed and woven" his life became. His dream of spring ". . . seemed suddenly, monotonously, attenuated. . . ." There were "no hands waving" to rescue him. Spring, the reader senses, has unaccountably failed the poet.

Yusef Komunyakaa's view of spring takes place up close and personal, with lively details of a chameleon poised on a shedded snakeskin, the whooping calls of quail, kudzu vines that "leapt blacktop, / snuck down back alleys," and so on. But he is quick to see realities others gloss over. It may be spring in Louisiana, but "[w]hat April couldn't fix / Wasn't worth the time. . . . A nest / of small deaths among anemone. . . . The struggle underneath / As if it never happened."

Of the four seasons, perhaps the most often written about, spring has inspired a huge assortment of poems, good and bad. Not all of the good ones could possibly fit into this anthology. Readers may be inspired to discover on their own the great British poets Wordsworth, Shelley, Keats, and Robert Herrick. On the other hand, there are many unexpected bonuses in the table of contents. I invite readers to open this volume and begin to experience the mesmerizing language of spring.

The Language of Spring

Metamorphosis

Always it happens when we are not there—
The tree leaps up alive into the air,
Small open parasols of Chinese green
Wave on each twig. But who has ever seen
The latch sprung, the bud as it burst?
Spring always manages to get there first.

Lovers of wind, who will have been aware
Of a faint stirring in the empty air,
Look up one day through a dissolving screen
To find no star, but this multiplied green,
Shadow on shadow, singing sweet and clear.
Listen, lovers of wind, the leaves are here!

Equinox

'. . . the sun crosses the equator
and day and night are equal'

My young-country is night
this minute and the cold
calls itself Spring, the sheep shift
rubbing their moony curls
or suckling in close-fenced fields
and a dog ratting the hayloft
speaks a perspective for quiet.

I elbow my desk in a glow
of yellow reflection: slant sun
and the immigrant leaves piling down.
Parrots flock out, somebody's
saw growls through the trees
and I curl a few words into fleece
to comfort what's cold in the bone.

PHILIP LARKIN

The Trees

The trees are coming into leaf
Like something almost being said;
The recent buds relax and spread,
Their greenness is a kind of grief.

Is it that they are born again
And we grow old? No, they die too.
Their yearly trick of looking new
Is written down in rings of grain.

Yet still the unresting castles thresh
In fullgrown thickness every May.
Last year is dead, they seem to say,
Begin afresh, afresh, afresh.

Vernal Sentiment

Though the crocuses poke up their heads in the usual places,
The frog scum appear on the pond with the same froth of
    green,
And boys moon at girls with last year's fatuous faces,
I never am bored, however familiar the scene.

When from under the barn the cat brings a similar litter,—
Two yellow and black, and one that looks in between,—
Though it all happened before, I cannot grow bitter:
I rejoice in the spring, as though no spring ever had been.

Relearning the Language of April

Where this man walks his fences
the willows do pliés with green laces,
eyelashes fly from the white plums,
the gaunt elms begin to open their frames.

When he passes, lithe with morning,
the terriers, rump-deep in a chuckhole,
boom out to follow,
the squirrels chirrup like cardinals.

Five prick-eared ponies
lift from their serious chewing.
The doomed cattle, wearing
intelligent smiles, turn.

For miles around, the plowed fields
release a sweet rancidness
warm as sperm.

I lie in the fat lap of noon
overhearing the doves' complaint.
Far off, a stutter of geese raise alarms.

Once more, Body, Old Paint,
how could you trick me like this
in spring's blowzy arms?

Late Snow

It's frail, this spring snow, it's pot cheese
packing down underfoot. It flies out of the trees
at sunrise like a flock of migrant birds.
It slips in clumps off the barn roof,
wingless angels dropped by parachute.
Inside, I hear the horses knocking
aimlessly in their warm brown lockup,
testing the four known sides of the box
as the soul must, confined under the breastbone.
Horses blowing their noses, coming awake,
shaking the sawdust bedding out of their coats.
They do not know what has fallen
out of the sky, colder than apple bloom,
since last night's hay and oats.
They do not know how satisfactory
they look, set loose in the April sun,
nor what handsprings are turned under
my ribs with winter gone.

Vernal Equinox

The scent of hyacinths, like a pale mist, lies between me
    and my book;
And the South Wind, washing through the room,
Makes the candles quiver.
My nerves sting at a spatter of rain on the shutter,
And I am uneasy with the thrusting of green shoots
Outside, in the night.

Why are you not here to overpower me with your tense
    and urgent love?

[in Just-]

in Just-
spring   when the world is mud-
luscious the little
lame balloonman

whistles   fat   and wee

andrunning from marbles and
piracies and it's
spring

when the world is puddle-wonderful

the queer
old balloonman
fat   and   wee
and bettyandisbel come dancing

from hop-scotch and jump-rope and

it's
spring
and
    the

       goat-footed

balloonMan   whistles
far
and
wee

April's Anarchy

All five shades of chameleon
Came alive on the cross-hatched
Snakeskin, & a constellation
Of eyes flickered in the thicket
As quail whooped up from sagebrush.
I duck-walked through mossy slag

Where a turtledove's call
Held daylight to the ground.
Vines climbed barbed wire
& leapt blacktop,
Snuck down back alleys,
Disguised with white blossoms,
Just to get a stranglehold
On young Judas trees.
Thorns nicked my left ear.
A hum rushed through leaves
Like something I could risk
Putting my hands on.
What April couldn't fix
Wasn't worth the time:
Egg shell & dried placenta
Light as memory.
Patches of fur, feathers,

& bits of skin. A nest
Of small deaths among anemone.
A canopy edged over, shadowplaying
The struggle underneath
As if it never happened.

Out of May's Shows Selected

Apple orchards, the trees all cover'd with blossoms;
Wheat fields carpeted far and near in vital emerald green;
The eternal, exhaustless freshness of each early morning;
The yellow, golden, transparent haze of the warm
    afternoon sun;
The aspiring lilac bushes with profuse purple or white
    flowers.

Touch of Spring

Thin wind winds off the water,
earth lies locked in dead snow,
but sun slants in under the yew hedge,
and the ground there is bare,
with some green blades there,
and my cat knows,
sharpening her claws on the flesh-pink wood.

Spring Changes

The autumnal drone of my neighbor
cutting wood across the pond
and the soundlessness of winter
give way to hammering. Must be
he's roofing, or building a shed
or fence. Some form of spring-induced
material advance.

Mother called early to say she's sold the house.
I'll fly out, help her sort and pack,
and give and throw away. One thing I'd like:
the yellow hand-painted pottery
vase that's crimped at the edge
like the crust of a pie—so gay, but
they almost never used it, who knows why?

A new young pair will paint and mow,
and fix the picket fence, wash windows face
to face in May, he outside on a ladder,
she inside on a chair, mouthing kisses
and "Be Careful!" through the glass.

Spring Was Begging to Be Born

After a winter of seclusion
I curtsy farewell to my pagoda:
Friend, tinfoil gangster, deviant silo,
I leave you to your own stale resources
to wander this spring in my disguises,
in my new naked zigzagging across
the pulsating battlefields of my own kind.

Murmur of cherry blossoms, I winced, glassy-eyed:
Had not I dreamed their color in my fairy tale?
Then hush; homeless now, I am arriving
at my one true home, the barricades melting.
The further I delved into these murderous zones
the more crisscrossed and woven became
the life within my fussy warehouse and that
beside this celebrated outer cherry.

Your wish is my command, I said to no one special.
Feeling festive now, and somewhat fraudulent,
I waited for the zodiac to sneak a glance
at my horoscope. Was this to be, spluttering,
with the plumes of raspberry light
erasing my hearsay and stifling my double?
I picked a thread from the zillion squiggles

and followed it around the corner to where
an orchestra was looking askance and
asking for complete silence.

Men sat outside their factories playing dominoes.
Their bodies were swollen, as after a hurricane.
I had dreamed of this hour; and yet, standing there,
my dream seemed suddenly, monotonously, attenuated,
as though a tugboat were the wiser to ignore
this sinking ship. I moved on, sobbing, giggling,
and looked back more than once to no hands waving.
Spring was truly begging to be born
like a cipher that aspires to the number one.
Hush. It is all hearsay, irresistible hearsay.

At April

Toss your gay heads,
    Brown girl trees;
Toss your gay lovely heads;
Shake your downy russet curls
All about your brown faces;
Stretch your brown slim bodies;
Stretch your brown slim arms;
Stretch your brown slim toes.
Who knows, better than we,
With the dark, dark bodies,
What it means
When April comes alaughing and aweeping
Once again
At our hearts?

April 5, 1974

The air was soft, the ground still cold.
In the dull pasture where I strolled
Was something I could not believe.
Dead grass appeared to slide and heave,
Though still too frozen-flat to stir,
And rocks to twitch, and all to blur.
What was this rippling of the land?
Was matter getting out of hand
And making free with natural law?
I stopped and blinked, and then I saw
A fact as eerie as a dream.
There was a subtle flood of steam
Moving upon the face of things.
It came from standing pools and springs.
And what of snow was still around;
It came of winter's giving ground
So that the freeze was coming out,
As when a set mind, blessed by doubt,
Relaxes into mother-wit.
Flowers, I said, will come of it.

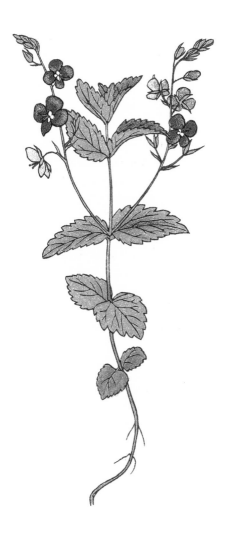

It Is a Spring Afternoon

Everything here is yellow and green.
Listen to its throat, its earthskin,
the bone dry voices of the peepers
as they throb like advertisements.
The small animals of the woods
are carrying their deathmasks
into a narrow winter cave.
The scarecrow has plucked out
his two eyes like diamonds
and walked into the village.
The general and the postman
have taken off their packs.
This has all happened before
but nothing here is obsolete.
Everything here is possible.

Because of this
perhaps a young girl has laid down
her winter clothes and has casually
placed herself upon a tree limb
that hangs over a pool in the river.
She has been poured out onto the limb,
low above the houses of the fishes
as they swim in and out of her reflection
and up and down the stairs of her legs.

Her body carries clouds all the way home.
She is overlooking her watery face
in the river where blind men
come to bathe at midday.

Because of this
the ground, that winter nightmare,
has cured its sores and burst
with green birds and vitamins.
Because of this
the trees turn in their trenches
and hold up little rain cups
by their slender fingers.
Because of this
a woman stands by her stove
singing and cooking flowers.
Everything here is yellow and green.

Surely spring will allow
a girl without a stitch on
to turn softly in her sunlight
and not be afraid of her bed.
She has already counted seven
blossoms in her green green mirror.
Two rivers combine beneath her.
The face of the child wrinkles
in the water and is gone forever.

The woman is all that can be seen
in her animal loveliness.
Her cherished and obstinate skin
lies deeply under the watery tree.
Everything is altogether possible
and the blind men can also see.

From you have I been absent...

From you have I been absent in the spring,
When proud-pied April (dress'd in all his trim)
Hath put a sprit of youth in every thing,
That heavy Saturn laugh'd and leapt with him.
Yet nor the lays of birds, nor the sweet smell
Of different flowers in odor, and in hue,
Could make me any summer's story tell,
Or from their proud lap pluck them where they grew;
Nor did I wonder at the lily's white,
Nor praise the deep vermilion in the rose,
They were but sweet, but figures of delight,
Drawn after you, you pattern of all those.
    Yet seem'd it winter still, and, you away,
      As with your shadow I with these did play.

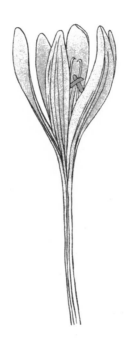

This Fevers Me

This fevers me, this sun on green,
On grass glowing, this young spring.
The secret hallowing is come,
Regenerate sudden incarnation,
Mystery made visible
In growth, yet subtly veiled in all,
Understandable in grass,
In flowers, and in the human heart,
This lyric mortal loveliness,
The earth breathing, and the sun.
The young lambs sport, none udderless.
Rabbits dash beneath the brush.
Crocuses have come; wind flowers
Tremble against quick April.
Violets put on the night's blue,
Primroses wear the pale dawn,
The gold daffodils have stolen
From the sun. New grass leaps up;
Gorse yellows, starred with day;
The willow is a graceful dancer
Poised; the poplar poises too.
The apple takes the seafoam's light,
And the evergreen tree is densely bright.
April, April, when will he
Be gaunt, be old, who is so young?
This fevers me, this sun on green,
On grass glowing, this young spring.

Eyesight

It was May before my
attention came
to spring and

my word I said
to the southern slopes
I've

missed it, it
came and went before
I got right to see:

don't worry, said the mountain,
try the later northern slopes
or if

you can climb, climb
into spring: but
said the mountain

it's not that way
with all things, some
that go are gone

Spring

Somewhere
  a black bear
    has just risen from sleep
      and is staring

down the mountain.
  All night
    in the brisk and shallow restlessness
      of early spring

I think of her,
  her four black fists
    flicking the gravel,
      her tongue

like a red fire
  touching the grass,
    the cold water.
      There is only one question:

how to love this world.
  I think of her
    rising
      like a black and leafy ledge

to sharpen her claws against
the silence
of the trees.
Whatever else

my life is
with its poems
and its music
and its glass cities,

it is also this dazzling darkness
coming
down the mountain,
breathing and tasting;

all day I think of her—
her white teeth,
her wordlessness,
her perfect love.

It's Spring Returning, . . .

It's spring returning, it's spring and love!
The buds, the birds, are about, above.
    Spring, and the joy it's bringing!
There's many a daisy down the dale,
Many a gala nightingale,
    Many a songbird singing.
The thrush is spunky and says his say,
Now woes of the winter wear away;
    And sprigs of the mint are springing.
The birds are flocking—afield, afar—
To tell high heaven how glad they are
    And set the woodland ringing.

The rose is swank in her rosy hood;
The leaves are a-sparkle in the wood
    And grow out green with a will.
The moon is sending us word she's bright;
The lily-flower is the day's delight.
    There's fennel and thyme and dill.
It's wooing time for the duck and drake;
Four-footed things, for their favorite's sake,
    Purr soft as a brook half-still.
The lover's moody—and others too;
I grant I'm a grumbler with that crew
    Who grieve for love grown chill.

The moon up there—she's a shining one!
By day there's the ever-splendid sun,
    And birds stir perkily.
There's dew a-dowsing the upland runs;
The wild things, gifted with mystic tongues,
    Speak forest policy.
Worms cuddle close in their clammy haunt;
Women, proud of their beauty, flaunt
    That pride—fine sight to see!
I'll have my way with a certain one,
Or all my joy in the world is done.
    It's off in the woods for me.

Song

It is not now I learn
To turn the heart away
From the rain of a wet May
Good for the grass and leaves.
Years back I paid my tithe
And earned my salt in kind,
And watched the long slow scythe
Move where the grain is lined,
And saw the stubble burn
Under the darker sheaves.
Whatever now must go
It is not the heart that grieves.
It is not the heart—the stock,
The stone,—the deaf, the blind—
That sees the birds in flock
Steer narrowed to the wind.

D. H. LAWRENCE

The Enkindled Spring

This spring as it comes bursts up in bonfires green,
Wild puffing of green-fire trees, and flame-green bushes,
Thorn-blossom lifting in wreaths of smoke between
Where the wood fumes up, and the flickering, watery rushes.

I am amazed at this spring, this conflagration
Of green fires lit on the soil of earth, this blaze
Of growing, these smoke-puffs that puff in wild gyration,
Faces of people blowing across my gaze!

And I, what sort of fire am I among
This conflagration of spring? the gap in it all—!
Not even palish smoke like the rest of the throng.
Less than the wind that runs to the flamy call!

The White Fury of the Spring

Oh, now, now the white fury of the spring
Whirls at each door, and on each flowering plot—
The pear, the cherry, the grave apricot!
The lane's held in a storm, and is a thing
To take into a grave, a lantern-light
To fasten there, by which to stumble out,
And race in the new grass, and hear about
The crash of bough with bough, of white with white.
Were I to run, I could not run so fast,
But that the spring would overtake me still;
Halfway I go to meet it on the stair
For certainly it will rush in at last,
And in my own house seize me at its will,
And drag me out to the white fury there.

The Widow's Lament in Springtime

Sorrow is my own yard
where the new grass
flames as it has flamed
often before but not
with the cold fire
that closes round me this year.
Thirtyfive years
I lived with my husband.
The plumtree is white today
with masses of flowers.
Masses of flowers
loaded the cherry branches
and color some bushes
yellow and some red
but the grief in my heart
is stronger than they
for though they were my joy
formerly, today I notice them
and turned away forgetting.
Today my son told me
that in the meadows,
at the edge of the heavy woods
in the distance, he saw
trees of white flowers.

I feel that I would like
to go there
and fall into those flowers
and sink into the marsh near them.

Spring

Nothing is so beautiful as spring—
   When weeds, in wheels, shoot long and lovely and lush;
   Thrush's eggs look little low heavens, and thrush
Through the echoing timber does so rinse and wring
The ear, it strikes like lightnings to hear him sing;
   The glassy peartree leaves and blooms, they brush
   The descending blue; that blue is all in a rush
With richness; the racing lambs too have fair their fling.

What is all this juice and all this joy?
   A strain of the earth's sweet being in the beginning
In Eden garden.—Have, get, before it cloy,
   Before it cloud, Christ, lord, and sour with sinning,
Innocent mind and Mayday in girl and boy,
   Most, O maid's child, thy choice and worthy the winning.

A Cold Spring

For Jane Dewey, Maryland
Nothing is so beautiful as spring. —Hopkins

A cold spring:
the violet was flawed on the lawn.
For two weeks or more the trees hesitated;
the little leaves waited,
carefully indicating their characteristics.
Finally a grave green dust
settled over your big and aimless hills.
One day, in a chill white blast of sunshine,
on the side of one a calf was born.
The mother stopped lowing
and took a long time eating the after-birth,
a wretched flag,
but the calf got up promptly
and seemed inclined to feel gay.

The next day
was much warmer.
Greenish-white dogwood infiltrated the wood,
each petal burned, apparently, by a cigarette butt;
and the blurred redbud stood
beside it, motionless, but almost more
like movement than any placeable color.
Four deer practised leaping over your fences.

The infant oak-leaves swung through the sober oak.
Song-sparrows were wound up for the summer,
and in the maple the complementary cardinal
cracked a whip, and the sleeper awoke,
stretching miles of green limbs from the south.
In his cap the lilacs whitened,
then one day they fell like snow.
Now, in the evening,
a new moon comes.
The hills grow softer. Tufts of long grass show
where each cow-flop lies.
The bull-frogs are sounding,
slack strings plucked by heavy thumbs.
Beneath the light, against your white front door,
the smallest moths, like Chinese fans,
flatten themselves, silver and silver-gilt
over pale yellow, orange, or gray.
Now, from the thick grass, the fireflies
begin to rise:
up, then down, then up again:
lit on the ascending flight,
drifting simultaneously to the same height,
—exactly like the bubbles in champagne.
—Later on they rise much higher.
And your shadowy pastures will be able to offer
these particular glowing tributes
every evening now throughout the summer.

EMILY DICKINSON

A Light exists in Spring

A Light exists in Spring
Not present on the Year
At any other period—
When March is scarcely here

A Color stands abroad
On Solitary Fields
That Science cannot overtake
But Human Nature feels.

It waits upon the Lawn,
It shows the furthest Tree
Upon the furthest Slope you know
It almost speaks to you.

Then as Horizons step
Or Noons report away
Without the Formula of sound
It passes and we stay—

A quality of loss
Affecting our Content
As Trade had suddenly encroached
Upon a Sacrament.

A little Madness in the Spring

A little Madness in the Spring
Is wholesome even for the King,
But God be with the Clown—

Who ponders this tremendous scene—
This whole Experiment of Green—
As if it were his own!

English Sparrows

(Washington Square)

How sweet the sound in the city an hour before sunrise,
When the park is empty and grey and the light clear and
      so lovely
I must sit on the floor before my open window for an
      hour with my arms on the sill
And my cheek on my arm, watching the spring sky's
Soft suffusion from the roofed horizon upward with
      palest rose,
Doting on the charming sight with eyes
Open, eyes closed;
Breathing with quiet pleasure the cool air cleansed by
      the night, lacking all will
To let such happiness go, nor thinking the least thing ill
In me for such indulgence, pleased with the day and with
      myself.
      How sweet
The noisy chirping of the urchin sparrows from crevice
      and shelf
Under my window, and from down there in the street,
Announcing the advance of the roaring competitive day
      with city bird-song.

Done With

My house is torn down—
Plaster sifting, the pillars broken,
Beams jagged, the wall crushed by the bulldozer.
The whole roof has fallen
On the hall and the kitchen
The bedrooms, the parlor.

They are trampling the garden—
My mother's lilac, my father's grapevine,
The freesias, the jonquils, the grasses.
Hot asphalt goes down
Over the torn stems, and hardens.

What will they do in springtime
Those bulbs and stems groping upward
That drown in earth under the paving,
Thick with sap, pale in the dark
As they try the unrolling of green.

May they double themselves
Pushing together up to the sunlight,
May they break through the seal stretched above them
Open and flower and cry we are living.

Naming of Parts

Today we have naming of parts. Yesterday,
We had daily cleaning. And tomorrow morning,
We shall have what to do after firing. But today,
Today we have naming of parts. Japonica
Glistens like coral in all of the neighboring gardens,
    And today we have naming of parts.

This is the lower sling swivel. And this
Is the upper sling swivel, whose use you will see,
When you are given your slings. And this is the piling swivel,
Which in your case you have not got. The branches
Hold in the gardens their silent, eloquent gestures,
    Which in our case we have not got.

This is the safety-catch, which is always released
With an easy flick of the thumb. And please do not let me
See anyone using his finger. You can do it quite easy
If you have any strength in your thumb. The blossoms
Are fragile and motionless, never letting anyone see
    Any of them using their finger.

And this you can see is the bolt. The purpose of this
Is to open the breech, as you see. We can slide it
Rapidly backwards and forwards: we call this

Easing the spring. And rapidly backwards and forwards
   The early bees are assaulting and fumbling the flowers:
      They call it easing the Spring.

   They call it easing the Spring: it is perfectly easy
   If you have any strength in your thumb: like the bolt,
   And the breech, and the cocking-piece, and the point of
         balance,
   Which in our case we have not got; and the almond-
         blossom
   Silent in all of the gardens and the bees going backwards
         and forwards,
      For today we have naming of parts.

There Will Come Soft Rains

(War Time)

There will come soft rains and the smell of the ground,
And swallows circling with their shimmering sound;

And frogs in the pools singing at night,
And wild plum-trees in tremulous white;

Robins will wear their feathery fire
Whistling their whims on a low fence-wire;

And not one will know of the war, not one
Will care at last when it is done.

Not one would mind, neither bird nor tree
If mankind perished utterly;

And Spring herself, when she woke at dawn,
Would scarcely know that we were gone.

Spring in New Hampshire

Too green the springing April grass,
  Too blue the silver-speckled sky,
For me to linger here, alas,
  While happy winds go laughing by,
Wasting the golden hours indoors,
Washing windows and scrubbing floors.

Too wonderful the April night,
  Too faintly sweet the first May flowers,
The stars too gloriously bright,
  For me to spend the evening hours,
When fields are fresh and streams are leaping,
Wearied, exhausted, dully sleeping.

Another Spring

If I might see another Spring,
    I'd not plant summer flowers and wait:
I'd have my crocuses at once,
My leafless pink mezereons,
      My chill-veined snowdrops, choicer yet
      My white or azure-violet,
Leaf-nested primrose; anything
      To blow at once, not late.

If I might see another Spring,
    I'd listen to the daylight birds
That build their nests and pair and sing,
Nor wait for mateless nightingale;
      I'd listen to the lusty herds,
      The ewes with lambs as white as snow,
I'd find out music in the hail
      And all the winds that blow.

If I might see another Spring—
    Oh stinging comment on my past
That all my past results in "if"—
      If I might see another Spring
I'd laugh to-day, to-day is brief;
I would not wait for anything:
      I'd use to-day that cannot last,
      Be glad to-day and sing.

Mauve

Last night a few beads or half-
moon spots in the grass
prophesied this shining. Reflections wink
on leaf and blade that the wind tips;
the glint of their fresh life is soft.
It is the moment of spring mauve
when certain tulips, ajuga,
and species bleeding-heart offer together,
blued down from frank pink, their
cups spikes and two-centered
flimsy bells. They rise a little
above the new green, and tilt
in the water-sounding air
full of lilac fall.

It could be any year of the last fifty
that I move among them (we never lose
our first lilacs; I stir here
and up absent avenues
layers of that smell drift,
under this smell, magnetic) as if
as once I were ignorant
not of doing
but of knowing
after having to.

Loveliest of trees, the cherry now

Loveliest of trees, the cherry now
Is hung with bloom along the bough,
And stands about the woodland ride
Wearing white for Eastertide.

Now, of my threescore years and ten,
Twenty will not come again,
And take from seventy springs a score,
It only leaves me fifty more.

And since to look at things in bloom
Fifty springs are little room,
About the woodlands I will go
To see the cherry hung with snow.

Selected Haiku

8

O finicky cat,
Forgive me for this spring rain
That disgusts you so!

79

Spring arrives stealthily:
Scaly flecks of peeling paint
On a whitewashed wall.

422

My cigarette glows
Without my lips touching it,—
A steady spring breeze.

A Prayer in Spring

Oh, give us pleasure in the flowers today;
And give us not to think so far away
As the uncertain harvest; keep us here
All simply in the springing of the year.

Oh, give us pleasure in the orchard white,
Like nothing else by day, like ghosts by night;
And make us happy in the happy bees,
The swarm dilating round the perfect trees.

And make us happy in the darting bird
That suddenly above the bees is heard,
The meteor that thrusts in with needle bill,
And off a blossom in mid air stands still.

For this is love and nothing else is love,
The which it is reserved for God above
To sanctify to what far ends He will,
But which it only needs that we fulfill.

Hold April

Hold on to April; never let her pass!
Another year before she comes again
To bring us wind as clean as polished glass
And apple blossoms in soft, silver rain.
Hold April when there's music in the air,
When life is resurrected like a dream,
When wild birds sing up flights of windy stair
And bees love alder blossoms by the stream.
Hold April's face close yours and look afar,
Hold April in your arms in dear romance;
While holding her look to the sun and star
And with her in her faerie dreamland dance.
Do not let April go but hold her tight,
Month of eternal beauty and delight.

Although he wrote poems on just about every topic under the sun, **A. R. Ammons** (1926–2001) was especially sensitive to the outdoor world—the seasons, the weather, the woods, the endless varieties of sky above. His keen love of nature is reflected in many of the titles he gave his collections: *Expressions of Sea Level* (1964), *Uplands* (1970), *The Snow Poems* (1977), *A Coast of Trees* (1981), and *Lake-Effect Country* (1983). Raised on a North Carolina farm, Ammons graduated from Wake Forest University with a degree in science. The recipient of numerous awards, including two National Book Awards and a MacArthur fellowship, Ammons taught at Cornell University from 1964 until his retirement in 1998. "Eyesight" appeared in *Briefings* (1971).

Elizabeth Bishop (1911–1979) grew up without parents and with no fixed location; her father died before she was a year old, and after her mother's breakdown and permanent institutionalization a few years later she was raised by various relatives in Massachusetts and Nova Scotia. She graduated from Vassar in 1934 and traveled widely, publishing her first poems in the late 1930s, which led to her first collection, *North & South,* in 1946. That volume introduced the geographical themes that continually fired her imagination. Bishop lived in Brazil from 1951 to 1970 (when she began teaching poetry at Harvard) and published several of her major volumes during this period: the Pulitzer Prize–winning *A Cold Spring* (1955), *Questions of Travel* (1965), and *The Complete Poems* (1969), which won the National Book Award.

A longtime poetry reviewer for *The New Yorker,* **Louise Bogan** (1897–1970) earned a serious reputation as both a critic and a poet. Born in Maine and educated in Boston schools, she married in 1916, and within a few years had a child, separated, and moved to Greenwich Village, where she formed associations with various literary groups and magazines and became one of the earliest Americans to undergo intensive psychoanalytic treatment, therapy she continued throughout her life. Her collections include *Body of this Death* (1923), *Dark Summer* (1929), *The Sleeping Fury* (1937), and *The Blue Estuaries: Poems 1923–1968* (1968).

The son of a Unitarian minister, **e. e. cummings** (1894–1962) was born in Cambridge, Massachusetts, and received his B.A and M.A. at Harvard, where he acquired modernist tastes and where his more conventional father taught English and ethics. Cummings's bohemian sensibilities were furthered encouraged by several years in Paris, where he lived after enlisting in an ambulance corps during World War I and then—suspected of spying—spending a few months in a French internment camp, an experience he memorably reported in *The Enormous Room* (1922). A talented painter, he moved in 1924 to Greenwich Village in hopes of becoming an artist but soon discovered he could also apply his visual gifts and experimental disposition to the shape of the poem on the printed page. "[In Just-]" was included in his first collection, *Tulips & Chimneys* (1923). *The Complete Poems* appeared in 1972.

Emily Dickinson (1830–1886) spent practically her entire life as a recluse in her parents' home in Amherst, Massachusetts, where her father served as treasurer of Amherst College. Although she wrote nearly two thousand poems, only a few were published in her lifetime. The first complete and textually authentic collection of her poetry did not appear until 1955, a publishing event that surely qualifies her as one of America's leading "modern" poets. Through uncanny paths of perception and with remarkable compression, her poems, like momentary flashes of insight, take us to the edges of human thought. Yet as enigmatic as these mental journeys may seem, they are firmly rooted in a particular place: "I see—New Englandly" she once rhymed.

Born into a prominent and prosperous Minnesota family in 1904, **Richard Eberhart** graduated from Dartmouth College in 1926 and did postgraduate work at Cambridge and Harvard. Eberhart worked at many odd jobs, one of them a *King & I* experience as the private tutor to the king of Siam's son. After naval service during World War II, he worked for several years in his wife's Boston family business but in the early 1950s began a lifetime of teaching at such colleges as Brown, Swarthmore, Tufts, Princeton, and Dartmouth, where he taught from 1956 to 1980. Eberhart published his first book of poetry, *A Bravery of Earth,* in 1931; in 1966 he won a Pulitzer Prize for his *Selected Poems* and in 1977 the National Book Award for *Collected Poems, 1930–1976.* His *New and Selected Poems* appeared in 1990.

"Spring is the mischief in me," writes **Robert Frost** (1874–1963) in "Mending Wall," one of his many poems celebrating the notoriously brief and ambivalent New England spring. So closely associated is Frost with New England that few people realize he was actually born in San Francisco. He didn't move east until he was eleven, when his father's death left the family penniless. "A Prayer in Spring" appeared in Frost's first poetry collection, *A Boy's Will* (1913), as part of a sequence of poems on youth; he had this to say in a note to the poem: the youth "discovers that the greatness of love lies not in forward-looking thoughts."

Angelina Weld Grimké (1880–1958) is best known as the author of *Rachel* (1916), one of the first successful African-American plays with an all-black cast. The daughter of a Harvard educated African-American lawyer and a prominent white Boston woman, Grimké was permanently abandoned by her mother, who could not withstand the social pressure of their interracial marriage, and raised solely by her father, who provided her with a solid private school education. Though she published poetry in some of the leading periodicals and anthologies connected with the Harlem Renaissance, her work remained uncollected until Carolivia Herron edited *Selected Works of Angelina Weld Grimké* in 1991.

When the poet Robert Bridges hesitantly edited and published the small posthumous volume of **Gerard Manley Hopkins's** *Poems* in 1918, he dramatically altered the course of modern poetry. Perhaps the most innovative Victorian poet, Hopkins (1844–1889) was born at Stratford in Essex and educated at Oxford, where he earned highest honors in classics and a reputation as a brilliant scholar. At Oxford he converted to Catholicism and in 1877 was ordained a Jesuit priest. Hopkins burned his early poetry when he entered religious life and his subsequent output was particularly small. He died of typhoid fever while a professor of classics at University College in Dublin.

After a poor showing in classics at Oxford, **A. E. Housman** (1859–1936) went on to publish brilliantly in the field and was made Professor of Latin at University College in London, where his scholarly reputation increased and eventually led to a prestigious position at Cambridge. He published only two thin volumes of poems in his lifetime—*A Shropshire Lad* (1896) and *Last Poems* (1922)—but their stoic lyricism and memorable phrasing attracted enormous attention and he became one of the most popular poets of his era; well into the 1960s his poetry was a staple of college admissions exams. For Housman, poetry was "not the thing said but a way of saying it."

Born in England in 1939 and educated at Cambridge University, where she received an M.A., **Aileen Kelly** has lived for most of her adult life in Melbourne, Australia. Widely published in Australian periodicals, she teaches adult education and is an active Roman Catholic, her work reflecting two strands of that tradition: a passion for social justice, and the incarnational spirituality called "nature mysticism." Her first book of poetry, *Coming Up* *for Light* (1994), won the prestigious Mary Gilmore Award from the Association for the Study of Australian Literature. She has spent time in Ireland, initially on a visit funded by the Vincent Buckley Poetry Award, which she received in 1998 from the University of Melbourne.

Born in 1947 in Ann Arbor, Michigan, **Jane Kenyon** graduated in 1970 from the University of Michigan, where she received an M.A. in 1972, the same year she married the poet Donald Hall, whom she had met as a student. They moved to Eagle Pond Farm in New Hampshire. Kenyon is the author of several volumes of poetry: *Constance* (1993), *Let Evening Come* (1990), *The Boat of Quiet Hours* (1986), and *From Room to Room* (1978). Her translation, *Twenty Poems of Anna Akhmatova,* was published in 1985. She was New Hampshire's poet laureate when she died of leukemia in 1995. *Otherwise: New and Selected Poems* appeared in 1996.

Yusef Komunyakaa, who has received numerous honors and awards, including a Pulitzer Prize for *Neon Vernacular* in 1994, the Ruth Lilly Poetry Prize in 2001, and a Bronze Star for service as a journalist in Vietnam, was born in Bogalusa, Louisiana, in 1947. His first book of poetry, *Dedications & Other Darkhorses,* appeared in 1977, and subsequent volumes include *Copacetic* (1984), *I Apologize for the Eyes in My Head* (1986), *Dien Cai Dau* (1988), *Magic City* (1992), *Thieves of Paradise* (1998), *Talking Dirty to the Gods* (2000), and *Pleasure Dome: New & Collected Poems, 1975–1999* (2001). He has written extensively on jazz and in 1999 was elected a chancellor of the Academy of American Poets. He lives in New York City and is a professor in the Council of Humanities and Creative Writing Program at Princeton University.

A longtime New Hampshire resident, where she raises horses and vegetables, **Maxine Kumin** was born in Philadelphia in 1925 and educated at Radcliffe College. Her books of poetry include *Connecting the Dots* (1996); *Looking for Luck* (1992); *Nurture* (1989); *The Long Approach* (1986); *Our Ground Time Here Will Be Brief* (1982); *The Retrieval Season* (1978); *House, Bridge, Fountain, Gate* (1975); and the Pulitzer Prize–winning *Up Country: Poems of New England* (1972). Besides novels, short stories, and several essay collections, she has also written many books for children. A poet laureate of New Hampshire, she has received an American Academy of Arts and Letters award, a National Endowment for the Arts grant, and fellowships from the Academy of American Poets and the National Council on the Arts. Her memoir *Inside the Halo and Beyond: The Anatomy of a Recovery* was published in 2000.

Named after the Renaissance poet Sir Philip Sidney, **Philip Larkin** (1922–1985) was born in Coventry, Warwickshire, and entered Oxford in 1940, escaping conscription because of his terrible eyesight. At Oxford he became close friends with the novelist Kingsley Amis and the two became influential members of a literary affiliation known as "The Movement." Reclusive and reluctant to read or lecture, Larkin worked most of his life as a librarian at the University of Hull. Each of his published volumes of poetry— among them *The North Ship* (1945), *The Less Deceived* (1955), *The Whitsun Weddings* (1964), and his final collection, *High Windows* (1974) —resonates with his remarkably understated wit and colloquial eloquence.

Known chiefly through such socially impassioned and sexually daring novels as *Sons and Lovers, The Rainbow, Women in Love, and Lady Chatterley's Lover,* **D. H. Lawrence** (1885–1930) began his literary career as a poet, publishing his first poems in a small magazine while he worked as a provincial schoolteacher. Lawrence grew up in a tense working-class family in Nottingham and received his education as a commuter at the University there. He is one of the first major British writers to find powerful sources of inspiration in classic American literature, especially in his poetry, which owes much to the rhythmical free verse of Walt Whitman. His first volume, *Love Poems and Others,* appeared in 1913 and was followed by over a dozen more, including a posthumous two-volume collection in 1939. *The Complete Poems* was published in three volumes in 1957.

A relative of James Russell Lowell, **Amy Lowell** (1874–1925) was born in Brookline, Massachusetts, the sister of Abbott Lawrence Lowell, who would serve as Harvard University's president for nearly twenty-five years. Influenced by the Imagist movement, she began publishing experimental and highly visual poems beginning with *Sword Blades and Poppy Seed* (1914). She became a leading and controversial advocate of the "New Poetry," which she helped promote through criticism, theatrical lecture tours, and collections. Her spirited but disorganized biographical study of John Keats appeared just before her untimely death. Though she received a posthumous Pulitzer Prize for her last volume of poetry, she remains a neglected literary figure, despite recent attention to feminist as well as gay and lesbian studies.

Claude McKay (1889–1948) was born in Jamaica into a large, poor family that managed to hold on proudly to its West African traditions. With the guidance of a British folklorist, the young McKay published two volumes of dialect verse that earned him sufficient prize money to study at Alabama's Tuskegee Institute, though after a few months he transferred to

Kansas State, where he studied agriculture for several years before moving to Harlem in 1914 and launching his literary career as one of the key members of the Harlem Renaissance. Associated with various radical publications, McKay spent a successful year in London, publishing in 1920 *Spring in New Hampshire,* a highly acclaimed volume introduced by the prominent British critic I. A. Richards. His next collection, *Harlem Shadows* (1922), contained an enormously popular sonnet that Winston Churchill once recited in an anti-Nazi address. Widely traveled and the author of a best-selling Harlem novel, McKay in 1944 converted to Catholicism in Chicago, where he had become closely involved with the National Catholic Youth Organization.

One of the most talked-about poets of the 1920s and thirties, **Edna St. Vincent Millay** (1892–1950) was born in Rockland, Maine, and educated at Vassar College, from which she graduated in 1917, the same year her first volume of poetry, *Renascence,* appeared to great acclaim. She moved to Greenwich Village, the stage for much of her highly publicized Bohemian life as well as her work. The next volumes came rapidly: *A Few Figs from Thistles* (1920), *Second April* (1921), and the Pulitzer Prize–winning *The Ballad of the Harp Weaver* (1922). She would publish many more collections, but her reputation as a lyricist rests primarily on these early books with their dominant fin de siècle theme of someone burning the candle at both ends. Her *Collected Poems* appeared posthumously in 1956.

Mary Oliver was born in 1935 in Maple Heights, Ohio. Her many books include *Winter Hours: Prose, Prose Poems, and Poems* (1999); *West Wind* (1997); *White Pine* (1994); *New and Selected Poems* (1992), winner of the National Book award; *House of Light* (1990), winner of the Christopher Award and the L. L. Winship/PEN New England Award; and *American Primitive* (1983), which won the Pulitzer Prize. She has also written *Rules for the Dance: A Handbook for Writing and Reading Metrical Verse* (1998); *Blue Pastures* (1995); and *A Poetry Handbook* (1994). She has received an American Academy of Arts and Letters Award, a Lannan Literary Award, and fellowships from the Guggenheim Foundation and the National Endowment for the Arts. She holds the Catharine Osgood Foster Chair for Distinguished Teaching at Bennington College.

Marie Ponsot's first book of poetry, *True Minds,* appeared in 1957 as the fifth volume in the famous City Lights Pocket Poets Series (Allen Ginsberg's *Howl* was Number Four). She did not publish a second collection until *Admit Impediments,* twenty-five years later. Born in New York City in 1921, she has translated dozens of books from the French and has received numerous awards, including the National Book Critics Circle Award for *The Bird Catcher* (1998), the Delmore Schwartz Memorial Prize, and the Shaughnessy Medal of the Modern Language Association. A teacher in the graduate writing program at Columbia University in New York City, she has published two other books of poetry, *The Green Dark* (1988) and *Springing: New and Selected Poems* (2002).

One problem in writing an unsurpassable poem is that the poet himself may never be able to surpass it. This apparently happened to **Henry Reed** (1914–1986), who long resented the fact that the enormous success of his "Naming of Parts" left him with the reputation as a "one-poem poet." The British poet, translator, critic, and famed radio dramatist—in 1947 he wrote for the BBC an award-winning dramatic version of *Moby Dick*—was born in Birmingham and gained his B.A. and M.A. at the university there. After serving in Army intelligence, Reed published *A Map of Verona* (1946), which included "Naming of Parts" along with several other war poems rooted in the vocabulary of military instruction. In 1970, Reed added a few more military poems and republished these as *The Lessons of War*. These remain his only volumes of poetry; his many radio dramas are published by the BBC.

Born in Maryland, **Lizette Woodworth Reese** (1856–1935) taught at various schools in the Baltimore area for forty-five years. She began publishing poetry in 1874 and her first volume, *A Branch of May*, which introduced her crisply drawn pastoral and springtime themes, appeared in 1887. Other volumes include *A Handful of Lavender* (1891), *A Quiet Road* (1896), *Spicewood* (1920), *Wild Cherry* (1923), *Selected Poems* (1926), *White April* (1930), *Pastures* (1933), and the posthumous verse narrative *The Old House in the Country* (1936). Reese also published two autobiographies, *A Victorian Village* (1920) and *The York Road* (1931).

Theodore Roethke (1908–1963) was born in Saginaw, Michigan, where his family owned an immense and profitable greenhouse and where he formed as a child the deep and mysterious attachment to the world of plants that pervades his poetry. After graduating from the University of Michigan in 1929, he studied briefly for an M.A. in English at Harvard but left to teach at Lafayette College, where he also coached varsity tennis. Although Roethke's teaching at a number of colleges was interrupted by several mental breakdowns, he published steadily and formed in the late forties a permanent association with the University of Washington in Seattle. *Open House,* his first collection, appeared in 1941 and was followed by *The Lost Son* (1948), *Praise to the End!* (1951), the Pulitzer Prize–winning *The*

Waking (1953), and *Words for the Wind* (1958), which won both the Bollingen Prize and the National Book Award. *The Far Field* was published posthumously in 1964.

Often considered the finest woman poet in English literature prior to the twentieth century, **Christina Georgina Rossetti** (1830–1894) was born into a highly cultured but financially strapped London family. She was educated at home by her half-English mother and Neapolitan refugee father, who eked out a living as an instructor of Italian. Fluent in English, Italian, French, German, and Latin, Christina Rossetti began writing poetry at an early age, as had her more famous brother Dante Gabriel. Reclusive, frequently ill, and a devout Anglican her entire life, she turned down two marriage proposals for religious reasons. Her major publications include *Goblin Market* (1862), *The Prince's Progress* (1866), *A Pageant* (1881), and *Verses* (1893).

A prolific poet, novelist, and memoirist, the Belgium-born **May Sarton** (1912–1995) came to the United States with her parents at the age of four to escape the Wehrmacht invasion. She grew up in Cambridge, Massachusetts, and published her first poetry at the age of seventeen, when she also left home to join New York's Civic Repertory Theater. In 1933, she founded her own repertory theater in Hartford, but when that failed, she left acting and returned to writing. Her first collection, *Encounter in April,* appeared in 1937 and was followed by over a dozen more volumes of poetry, numerous novels, and a handful of autobiographies. She taught at Harvard and Wellesley, before moving permanently to Maine in 1973. Her *Collected Poems* was published in 1993, shortly before she died of breast cancer.

Anne Sexton (1928–1974) was born in Newton, Massachusetts, and spent her entire life in the Boston vicinity. As a young woman she briefly modeled and—not possessing a college degree—studied poetry in adult education workshops, where she met Maxine Kumin, who would be a lifelong friend. Married at the age of twenty, she went through years of therapy with occasional institutionalization after several devastating mental breakdowns in the mid-fifties, stark experiences that form the core of her first award-winning volume of poetry, *To Bedlam and Part Way Back* (1960). Her stability worsened after her divorce in 1973 and not long afterward she committed suicide.

Unlike most of the poets included here, **William Shakespeare** (1564–1616) received no prestigious awards and earned no degrees but he nevertheless enjoyed financial success and thundering applause as a theatrical entrepreneur, an actor, and one of the most popular London playwrights of his time. The applause continues still and will undoubtedly never cease. Like the Beatles, who "discovered" rock and roll when the trend appeared to be over, Shakespeare saw his sonnet sequence published (without his consent) in 1609, long after such sequences were fashionable. By then he had already written nearly all of his major plays and was about to retire to his birthplace, Stratford. He was born in April and he died in April.

Ann Stanford (1916–1987) was born in California and educated at Stanford and UCLA, where she received her Ph.D. Her work deeply examines our relationship with nature and—as in "Done With"—often reveals the struggle between urban and natural processes. Her major books of poetry include *The Weathercock* (1966), *The Descent* (1970), and *In Mediterranean Air* (1977). She has translated *The Bhagavad Gita,* published a study of the Puritan poet Anne Bradstreet, and edited a landmark anthology, *The Women Poets in English.* She also served as poetry editor for the *Los Angeles Times* and chairperson for the Pulitzer Prize Committee. A collection of her later poems, *Dreaming the Garden,* appeared in 2000, and was followed a year later by a volume of poems selected by former students, *Holding Our Own.*

Jesse Stuart (1906–1984) was born in a log cabin in the Kentucky hills that he would one day celebrate in his poetry, fiction, and essays. One of the most popular short story writers of the forties and fifties, Stuart published his first book of verse, *Man with a Bull-Tongue Plow,* in 1934. A poet laureate of Kentucky, nearly all his work is rooted in the mountain country of his native state, a region he also lovingly describes in such autobiographical books as *Beyond Dark Hills* (1938) and *The Thread That Runs So True* (1949). The recipient of awards from the Guggenheim Foundation, the Academy of Arts and Science, and the Academy of American Poets, Stuart also wrote several extremely popular books for young people. A few of his later poetry collections are *Hold April* (1961), *Come, Gentle Spring* (1969), and *Dawn of Remembered Spring* (1972), titles that show Stuart's relevance to this anthology.

Soon after **James Tate**'s highly acclaimed first book of poetry, *The Lost Pilot,* appeared in 1967, he joined the faculty of the University of Massachusetts, Amherst, where he still teaches. Born in Kansas City, Missouri, in 1943, he has received many awards and honors, among them a National Institute of Arts and Letters Award for Poetry; the Wallace Stevens Award; fellowships from both the Guggenheim Foundation and the National Endowment for the Arts; the National Book Award, for *Worshipful Company of Fletchers* (1994); and a Pulitzer Prize, for *Selected Poems* (1991). Other volumes include *The Oblivion Ha-Ha* (1970), *Riven Doggeries*

(1979), *Distance from Loved Ones* (1990), and *Memoir of the Hawk* (2001). He currently serves as a chancellor of the Academy of American Poets.

Sara Teasdale (1884–1933) was born in St. Louis and like one of her favorite poets, Christina Rossetti, was largely educated at home. Her parents privately printed her first volume, *Sonnets to Duse* (1907), which was followed by *Helen of Troy* (1911) and *Rivers to the Sea* (1915). By this time she had become a frequent contributor to Harriet Monroe's influential *Poetry* magazine. In 1916 Teasdale moved with her husband to New York, where she received a special Pulitzer Prize for the highly successful *Love Songs* (1917) and edited one of the first collections of women's poetry, *The Answering Voice* (1917). Other volumes include *Flame and Shadow* (1920), *Dark of the Moon* (1926), and *Strange Victory* (1933), which appeared shortly after she killed herself with an overdose of sleeping pills.

One of the nation's most prolific and versatile writers, **John Updike** was born in Shillington, Pennsylvania, in 1932. After graduating from Harvard in 1954, he studied art at Oxford, and returned to take a job with *The New Yorker*, which he left after two years, moving to Massachusetts to pursue the "solitary trade" of a freelance writer. With over fifty books, two Pulitzer Prizes, a National Book Award, and a National Book Critics Circle award —besides many others—he surely gives the modest term "freelance writer" a new meaning. Besides his many novels (some of the most popular being the "Rabbit" series that began with *Rabbit, Run* in 1960), Updike has written much nonfiction, criticism, and poetry. His *Collected Poems* appeared in 1993 and his most recent volume is *Americana and Other Poems* (2001).

Walt Whitman (1819–1892) is America's national poet, the single voice that most fully represents the American experience. *Leaves of Grass,* the volume he labored, fussed, and fought over from the first privately printed edition in 1855 until the "deathbed edition" of 1892, remains the most influential work of poetry in American literary history. Born into a working-class Long Island family, Whitman grew up as a Quaker in Brooklyn, dropping out of school at eleven to find a trade. Like Benjamin Franklin and Mark Twain, he learned printing, a skill that landed him several newspaper positions as a reporter and editorial writer. When the 1882 edition of *Leaves of Grass* was suppressed in Boston, the publicity helped the volume earn its best sales ever, and Whitman was able to buy a small house in Camden, New Jersey, where he modestly entertained distinguished visitors from all over the world and cultivated the many myths that began flourishing about him well before his death.

Verbally polished until they shine, **Richard Wilbur**'s poems have served as models of the poet's craft ever since *The Beautiful Changes and Other Poems* appeared in 1947. One would be hard-pressed to find a reputable textbook on the art of poetry that did not include a few examples of Wilbur's disciplined and exemplary work. Born in New York City in 1921, Wilbur was educated at Amherst College (where he studied with Robert Frost) and Harvard University. America's Poet Laureate in 1987, Wilbur won the Pulitzer Prize in 1989 for his *New and Collected Poems*. He has taught for many years at Wesleyan University and is also well known for his highly acclaimed translations of Molière.

William Carlos Williams (1883–1963) worked hard all his life at two demanding careers: as a busy pediatrician in the densely populated, working-class area of Rutherford, New Jersey, where he was born, and as one of the leading figures of modern American poetry. Williams's mother was Puerto Rican and he grew up speaking Spanish. After receiving his medical education at the University of Pennsylvania, where he became friends with Ezra Pound, Williams returned to his hometown in 1910 and began practicing the arts of healing and writing. Published at his own expense, his first collection of poems was followed by nearly forty volumes of poetry, including *Spring & All* (1923), short stories, novels, history, criticism, drama, and autobiography. He received the National Book Award for his urban epic *Paterson* (1950) and a posthumous Pulitzer Prize for his final collection, *Pictures from Brueghel*, in 1963.

Richard Wright (1908–1960) was born into a Mississippi sharecropper family and after graduating from junior high school in 1925 joined the "great migration" to Chicago. He experimented with fiction, poetry, and politics, joining the Communist party in 1933, and four years later moved to Harlem to edit the *Daily Worker* and publish *Uncle Tom's Children: Four Novellas* (1938). His most successful book, *Native Son* (1940), the first book by an African American to be a Book of the Month Club selection, was followed by another best-seller, the autobiography *Black Boy* (1945). Disenchanted, Wright left the Communist Party in 1944 and in 1947 moved with his family permanently to Paris, where Jean-Paul Sartre introduced him to the existentialist philosophy that would inform his later books. In the final months of his life, Wright wrote some four thousand haiku, of which he selected 817 that were finally published in *Haiku: This Other World* in 1998.